Love's Bluff

Patti See

Plain View Press
P. O. 42255
Austin, TX 78704

plainviewpress.net
sbright1@austin.rr.com
1-512 441 2452
1-512-440-7139 (fax)

This book is a work of fiction. Some of these poems are autobiographical in form but not in fact. My family, neighbors and friends did not serve as models. PKS

Cover Art, *Eau Claire*, by Todd Clercx.

Contents

FACE-TO-FACE   9

Telling My Mother I Can't Say the Rosary   11
Suburbs, Summer 1972   13
Suburbs, Summer 1972   14
Suburbs, Summer 1972   15
Shotgun   16
Driftwood   18
Writing Down Your Bones   20
Billie Holiday at Dusk   21
Wanted   22
Haircut   23
Fifteen Reasons We Can't Have an
     Intelligent Discussion About *Gilligan's Island*   **25**
Soup's On   26
Alex Fighting Sleep   28
Love's Bluff   29
After the Dentist   30
All She Ever Wanted   31

COMMMUNAL   **33**

True Confessions   35
Man of the House   37
When the Search Committee Asks Me
     To Tell A Little About Myself   38
Scrubbing   40
"Life in These United States"   41
At the National Fresh Water Fishing
     Hall of Fame, Hayward, WI   42
Untitled (or What I Hate)   44
My Mother, According to Me   45
Two Houses Over   47
Saturn Send-Off   48
For Alex, At Ten   50
Love is Anticipation   51
Pop Quiz   52
Wedding Dance   53
Proposition   55
Found: Poem   57

Escape Fantasies   58
All She Ever Wanted   60

SCREENED   61

Nothing She Ever Wanted   63
Rewinding the Wedding Tape   64
Inamorata   65
Rapture of the Deep   66
Dumplings, A Family Recipe   67
What We've Seen: Bayfield, Wisconsin   69
What We've Seen: Bayfield, Wisconsin   70
What We've Seen: Bayfield, Wisconsin   71
April Rain   72
Couple   74
Passing   75
Thighs Like Fresh Peaches   76
Handbreadth Away   77
Three Cities Away   78
What She Wants to Know   79
All She Ever Wanted   80

About the Author   81
About the Artist   81

"Why don't you love me like you used to do
How come you treat me like a worn out shoe
My hair's still curly and my eyes are still blue
why don't you love me like you used to do?"
    – Hank Williams

Acknowledgments

Grateful acknowledgment to the following publications, in which versions of some of these poems first appeared:

Alternatives: Roads Less Traveled (Outrider Press): "Inamorata;" *Brevity: A Journal of Concise Literary Nonfiction:* "Suburbs, Summer 1972;" *California Quarterly:* "All She Ever Wanted;" *Evansville Review:* "At the National Fresh Water Fishing Hall of Fame, Hayward, WI;" *Gypsy Cab: An Anthology of Women Writers:* "Alex Fighting Sleep," "April Rain;" *Hamline Review:* "When the Search Committee. . . " and "Driftwood;" *HipMama:* "For Alex, at Ten;" *A More Perfect Union: Poems and Stories about the Modern Wedding* (St. Martin's Press): "Shotgun;" *The Mother is Me:* "Man of the House;" *Savoy Magazine:* "Billie Holiday at Dusk," "Passing," "Writing Down Your Bones;" *Sun Dog: The Southeast Review:* "True Confessions" (also anthologized in *Prairie Hearts: Women View the Midwest*, Outrider Press and *Upriver4*); *Red River Review:* "Scrubbing;" *Vestal Review:* "Thighs Like Fresh Peaches;" *Volume One:* "Escape Fantasies;" *Water-Stone* "Soup's On;" *Wisconsin Academy Review:* "Fifteen Reasons We Can't Have an Intelligent Discussion About Gilligan's Island" and "Proposition;" *Wisconsin English Journal:* "Handbreadth Away" and "Haircut;" *Women's Studies Quarterly:* "My Mother, According to Me."

I am forever grateful to:

Jeannette Prince who called me a poet in fifth grade, and Malcolm Mosing and Marty Crowe who ruined my life with literature. Thank you to friends and editors who saw many versions of these poems and set me straight — Carrie Butler Becker, Jayne Blodgett, Beth Bretl, Krista Clercx, Yvette Flaten, Art Lyons, Frank Smoot, and Bruce Taylor. Thank you to Alex who's been a joy to watch grow, Todd Clercx who captured the Joynt on canvas and so graciously allowed me to use his painting, and Susan Bright at Plain View Press.

You You You You You

FACE-TO-FACE

Telling My Mother I Can't Say the Rosary

"One may gain a partial indulgence for the Rosary's
recitation in whole or in part in other circumstances."
          How to Pray the Rosary

It was the UPS strike of '75, I say
pointing to the line of First Communion photos
holding up her living room.
Five sisters before me captured
in their portrait grace of Catholic girlhood
both brothers in plaid jackets and bow ties
against a starburst gray background
the girls set before the tunnel to paradise
in the same crepe paper dress and haloed veil
posed and boxed for two decades.

I wore the dress last, over my *Charlie's Angels*
tank top and running shorts in the June studio
with the borrowed prayer book and scapula
the hand-me-down rosary, my parcel
ransomed in some packed warehouse
my body not yet the Temple
my mother warned it would be
ankles crossed awaiting stigmata
that may appear, like the Holy Spirit,
at any moment. Or it was

the Lutheran convert Miss Rhinehart
who learned our prayers with us
her first-ever second grade class
accepted the alien ritual creeds, but could not
describe the wafer's sacred taste much less
name the Joyful, the Sorrowful, the Glorious.
She handed out dittoed examples of the Rosary
all winter blue bleeding to white
warning us not to sniff the fumes as we waited
for the Ugly Pickle Sucker's* deliverance.

Up and down tickle-belly orchard roads
we'd have surely crashed the paneled station wagon
if not for my mother's mumbling over glass beads
purer than her rounded-out trinket bought
at the *Passion Play* just past Davenport, Florida.
A knob for each decade surrounds the sterling crown
of thorns in my cupped hand, the ring topped
by the Crucifixion, on the other side tarnished
letters form *Ave Maria* with the Mother
of God assuming like mothers do.

The Evelyn Wood version, I ask
as she offers me her new treasure
compact as a travel cribbage board
more brass knuckle than absolution
more gewgaw than amulet. She slips
me the pamphlet *How to Pray the Rosary*
Cliff's notes for the religiously challenged
the Virgin Mary circled by diagrams and pagan
arrows, catechism quirky as Jumanji rules
more of the mystery we've become.

Now in my impiety I hide this promise

of redemption in my hip pocket
like an illiterate carrying Blake
what curse, what menat**

whatever the last little Glory be.

* slang for UPS drivers in elementary school circles
** ring or necklace that is believed to bring divine protection

Suburbs, Summer 1972

My mother starts each day with a cigarette from her Tupperware pouch
and the radio tuned to the polka station, where *fm* means *fine music*,
blaring from the kitchen window sill. Through our backyard, sun
gleams off of Mr. Schwan's lifetime collection of Air Streamers, where
thirty cats, some neighbors say, roam free. Next door on Lipinski's
weeping willow the Brenner boys in their ripped Toughskins, the
summer before reform school, swing across fence tops Tarzan-style
even before breakfast.

Our open curtains signal Pug Lipinski to part the lilac hedge and walk
around the shaded spot we all avoided from the summer Taffy coughed
up worms. He never knocks, just presses his face – streaked with this
morning's jelly or last night's gravy – on our screen door. He always has
a Tonka truck in one hand and an ice cream pail of army men in the
other. Bobby still plays with him even though it's the summer before
junior high. Next summer he'll be Rob and sulk around the basement
listening to KISS.

Suburbs, Summer 1972

She doesn't say so, but my mother hopes this is the last summer that
Mrs. Lipinski spends most days half in the bag, lying on the chaise
lounge, the only piece of living room furniture not covered in plastic,
and sipping coffee mugs of spiked orange juice. By nine she has
screamed her litany of *God damn you's* until all seven of her children
scattered. She'll be back in bed by noon claiming migraines, up by
suppertime with wet kisses for all the children, even the neighbor's.

My father wears his *again* face, home on his lunch break, each time
he passes half of the Lipinski kids eating Wonder bread and bologna
sandwiches on his picnic table. I hear my mother say to him once in
the kitchen, cutting more sandwiches into triangles, "Don't hold your
breath."

Suburbs, Summer 1972

It's the first summer that I ride the three blocks alone to Ludwig's for Lucky Strikes with the worn note for Mr. Ludwigson tucked in my sock beside two quarters fresh from my mother's gambling purse. I steer my banana-seat bike around pavement cracks as Old Maid cards click time clothes-pinned to spokes, gathering enough kids to divvy teams for kickball where Hoover and Garfield Streets form a T. The sewer grates become bases, that ragged car mat is always home plate, fouls are ticks and everyone calls do-overs. Skynard blasts from Mikey's blue ox blue Gran Torino as he hoses down his baby in our driveway, wondering who'll wash her when he leaves for boot camp. He still lets us shoot arrows at him till he sprays us, or he takes a turn pitching, and we all yell "we want a pitcher, not a belly itcher" for every bumpy one.

On hot days, Beth, exotic in her two-piece, lays-out topless on the garage roof, baby oil puddled in her belly button, sneaking Kools if I play lookout, which I always, always do. More than anything I want to look like her, or better, be her, the summer before she got her first job as a carhop at the Falls Drive-In and called me a pest. I don't know yet that it's the last summer she will fit in the pool with me, her bony limbs cracking the plastic.

So I look at Shelley Brenner, too dirty to dip into the calm waters of our fish-bottomed pool, even with the foot-wash bucket, as she sits on her curb and watches from across the street. And that's all I do that summer, just look back.

Shotgun

Early mornings the baby nudges
between us, what Dr. Spock warned
against and Donahue promoted
He pokes with straight toes
a fork to your knife and my spoon.
Together we are a set.

Mornings lately you watch us sleep
before your predictable peck good-bye.
Our son and I share one pillow.
His hair is the color of mine when we met
a girl in braces and Catholic plaid
wild blonde wisps barretted back.

In our other life you often watched me sleep.
Your look reminds me of mornings past
waking up on your couch
sneaking home before daylight
with my bra in my pocket
and whisker burns on my cheeks.

We were saving for a motorcycle
with a Colonel Klink sidecar.
I would ride shotgun on our
cross country trip for two.
Then our child was no more than a name
scrawled in a notebook margin

not this lump dividing us on cold mornings.
Once we wondered what people thought
a bride who wore white, a groom who wept
at the sight of her, a nine-pound preemie.
The three of us learn daily how
to crawl, to bite, to live, together.

Now nightly Colgate kisses replace
those Juicy Fruit mouths of dating
and your watching eyes question.
Some day with more small bodies
between us you'll see that my long arms
can reach out across our wealth

of feet-in pajamas. When you wake me.
And tonight before you carry
the groggy baby from his crib
to our bed I'll answer in riddle.
I care for each more than the other,
but you are not mine to mother.

Driftwood

"Today I discover I am not all wood."
– Anne Sexton

You move along the rocks
balancing our son on your back
as we traipse through the woods
you knew as a boy

searching for arrowheads
or making your own
scraping just right bits of shale
against these same rocks.

You know better
than your son's palm
this trail that in April is no more
no less than mud

guiding us along the creek's purl
to a hidden surprise
you tell him
a waterfall that today only drips.

Now your turf's a park where bankers
bring their children on Sundays
empty this Easter
but for speed walkers

and winter rubbish the river
eases back to its banks:
Coke cans, bits of cloth, a Wonder bag
and wood enough for a stick house.

Our son throws twigs the size of his fingers,
of his arms, finally the size of your calf
then races to the bridge to watch
his best throws pass us by.

Writing Down Your Bones

Cranium to occiput
lucky orbital cavity
aqueous and vitreous humor
holding what you see.

Propitious my words
slipping past vestibule to dull labyrinth
gong of your malleus
tympanic beats of your blood.

Mandible, maxilla
your sweet occlusion
slow rictus my fortunate hand quiets
stern gladiolus, tingling axilla, angelic scapula.

Felicitous crook of arm hooked between ulna
and crazy when tickled humorous
slim carpus, pubis to sacrum
ilium, ilia crest, ischium.

Rollicked coccyx holding you arched
O beaded sacral vertebrae
responsive sciatic alighting femur, fibula, tibia
thick tarsus, sturdy terminal digits
parted, tipping to me.

Billie Holiday at Dusk

Another night looms
without you
keeper of my feral dreams

another evening unraveling
at my feet the retinue
of your leaving

soothed only
by the honeyed gravel
of "You Thrill Me."

This rumination's too blue
too many love songs
too little you.

Wanted

Got kidney?
Kidney needed
Kidney desperately needed

Please help me to live
Let's meet on this side of heaven
Life Desired – Age 23

Baby needs healthy kidney
Dad of 14 year old needs a kidney
Young woman ready for new life

Looking for Kidney Angel
Yearning 4 an O+ kidney to fill my life's dreams
Appreciative of Kidney

Looking for any kidney
Desperately Need Your Help to Live
Angel with a kidney wanted

I'm in need of a kidney, please
Need a kidney – will you help?
My family needs me

NO NEED TO REPLY SON
PASSED AWAY ON 6/15/05

(Poem is made up of actual titles of patient profiles seeking kidney donors on
MatchingDonors.com.)

Haircut

Midsummer's child, splitting the season
like a halved watermelon, born
and celebrated when corn is just past

knee high. We prepare you for days,
telling you for this birthday you'll get
big boy cut. In the bath tub I stretch

your tight wet curls down the length
of your back as we pose
for one last pre-cut picture.

Then the three of us move to the patio;
you and I do the spider on a paint splattered
step stool. Your father, today's barber,

holds the awkward orange Fiskers
and a gap-toothed comb. At first
you still believe this gift is one we'll

open together. But even in your silence
you're contented with the promise
of a popsicle, grape not red. A Mowgli

beach towel is safety-pinned around
your angel bones, and underneath your
cape are Ninja Turtle underwear

with the crotch you've not yet mastered.
Your nails tell the story of many sandboxes.
The first snip is the hardest: where to begin

on this golden frenzied mop. Ringlets
the color of wheat in sun spring to
the ground and blow clump by clump

into the grass. For birds' nests my mother
would say, knowing better than I that
everything finds a home. Your remaining

hair recoils snug to your scalp like
a cartoon tongue rolling itself back in.
No more androgyny, my baby. Soon

preschool, then Little League, Boy Scouts.
No longer Shirley Temple to the blue
haired women at the market who ask

if *Mama does your hair.* Now with
the last of your baby loveliness cut
away, I save a handful of hair in a plastic

windowed business envelope
to seal in the urn your baby book has
become, knowing your hair will grow

back wavier, darker, coarser, never
nearly as soft. And at last, framing your
face in my hands—dreading the summer

day I'll need relics of you, I see
you for the first time, my son.

Fifteen Reasons We Can't Have an Intelligent Discussion About *Gilligan's Island*

for Bruce

You don't understand why any man wouldn't want to be king.
You think Hamlet shouldn't be a musical.
You never wanted to be Ginger but ended up the Professor.
You don't believe the cast is based on the seven deadly sins.

You don't know the Professor's name.
You've never contemplated why the Howells
took so much cash for a three hour trip.
You don't know where Mary Ann's from.

You're too contemporary to watch sitcoms that exploit
head hunters, near-sighted Japanese soldiers, and dyslexic pilots.
You're too passive aggressive to watch a grown man
strike another with his captain's hat.

You wonder if Gilligan ever left his hammock
or why the Professor roomed alone.
You ponder what Skipper meant by *Little Buddy*.
You still haven't gotten over Maynard G. Krebbs' cancellation.

You spent the seventies married
tying flies in your basement over a warm can of Schlitz.
I learned long division in front of the TV
humming *You're sure to get a smile*.

You spent the eighties at double bubble
rediscovering how to dance with a stranger.
I endured junior high's ugly years
with a predictable tune that soothed me through

dazed and clueless whistling each afternoon
This is the tale of our castaways.

Soup's On

Each supper time my father yells *Soup's on*
from the porch railing, comb over growing
in the night breeze, the rolled newspaper passed
to his half mooned arm pit. Nothing's worth
reading since Tricky Dick, but he'll laugh alone
at the comics. The neighborhood loved

his call. Other kids scrambled to hand over
toys and even parents thought we only ate soup.
Hungry, we'd say, darting home, hiding that he only
called once. He was the man of our world, grown
up and stern, who didn't know what play was worth
or couldn't afford to. Each of us passed

him on the porch with a nod as his eyes passed
over the sea of seven children he loved.
A man for whom words were worthless
found his way of saying I'm here. *Soup's on.*
We didn't know what could make a grown
man hate his life, believing that only

kids lost the power to please. He sat as if alone,
his spoon in one hand, back and forth, passing
bowl to lips, his free hand scribbling with a grown
up finger on the table top. If it was a meal he loved
—pig's feet with sauerkraut, tongue soup
with egg dumplings—it was a dish worthy

of *Wonder what the poor people are eating*, worth
a table laugh each time, the way that only
kids have to laugh at a father. He ate his soup
as he did everything, looking at the door past
us, his rhythmic dull at the machine motion, loving,
it seemed, only what he saw there, as we grew

up telling each other stories. Now we use grown
up words, though I can't tell him what's worthwhile
we often stumble upon, how I know silence is love
and words can't make it better, how lonely
fathers who yelled from porches too often slip past
us, how I still want to call back to him, *I'm on*

my way, how I've grown to know what to leave
alone and know what's worth passing on,
how I hold my son and say *Soup's on*.

Alex Fighting Sleep

"I
like you this much.
Big as this room
as this house and our yard
much as giants are big

I like
you this much
big as daddy's head
much as Grandma's bra
I like you

this much
big as Minnesota
much as all the stars
far as the Enterprise

through the universe
and back to Chippewa Falls."

Love's Bluff

"Well I remember every little thing as if it happened only yesterday.
Parking by the lake and there was not another car in sight."
— Meatloaf, "Paradise by the Dashboard Light"

Driving past another scenic overlook
your mind swerves to the boy you thought
you'd married. Car doors locked against hooked
strangers and cops, steaming windows, caught

in that lusty fascination. Your first sleep over
you smell his pillow when he's away,
talk each other to sleep under the covers.
Then the baby's wedged between all you say.

You're still spunky and he says you look
pretty good, and he's still nice, but overnight
you're more house manager than lover.
Lately he tells himself about his day.

You write poems about him, of course, and others
discover your knack for form and rhyme, he
asks between innings how to make it better.
You take classes, and he sets up a 401 K.

Once it didn't matter that he balls his socks
or that neither rake nor shovel nor rag fit
his hand or that you could nearly cook
just your mammalian ping, his tip

of tongue, how that dull rush endures.
You remember stumbling blindly through,
pulling into dead end nights only aging cures.

Believing in married love, like true
rhyme, you know, is for kids and amateurs.
Still you want to, you really do.

After the Dentist

There's a taste I don't quite know
bitter on the back of my tongue.
Our heads together on his pillow
I tell him I taste hygienist's gloves.
"What?" he says. "You taste like
balloons," I say. He's quiet.
"What do you think about that?"
"*I taste like balloons?* No one's
ever said that to me."

Maybe no one's ever said that to anyone.

All She Ever Wanted

A bathtub big enough for two, an oven that
makes its own casserole, a man who'd love
her reluctantly, a novel she could finish.

COMMMUNAL

True Confessions

The summer Coke changed its recipe back
to Classic and Sally Jesse Raphael moved from radio
to TV, I sweltered over a grill in the screened Falls
Drive-In kitchen turning burgers and dropping fries;
or I fitted trays to car windows, waiting for fifteen
to bump into sixteen and transform me from carhop

to sultry teen beauty. The Farrrah-haired carhops,
busty and tan, swiveled aprons and necks. Down my back
hung a kinky mop I'd hid behind for all of my fifteen
years. Most shifts I watched the highway, radios
blasting from cars driving past; or I memorized a fried
food litany: pizza burger, pronto pup, ribette – all falling

into a chain – zebra cone, slop, polar bear. Chippewa Falls
girls were separated, hot items from cold. An older carhop
told me dropping cheese curds into the deep fryer,
You Catholic girls have it easy, no guilt, just pay-back
with Novenas. I shrugged, listening for some distant radio.
A week later we guzzled Andre pink bought for $2.15

a bottle and closed Babe's Bar where even fifteen
was old enough. After my first acknowledged fall
it got easier to feign experience, turn up the radio
with public school boys and their dollar tips. I carhopped
the weeks away to Fridays, when I ran to the bank and back,
or face to face confessed my sins, still afraid of frying

in hell. The worst I penanced alone, silently deep frying
away with half-chicken Sunday dinners. At fifteen
a Hail Mary for every boy or Glory Be for every beer backed
up my lies quick as a reorder slip. I spent slow days at the Falls
playing tic-tac-toe alone and learned from the other carhops
that most boys were really not the heroes that made radio

love songs, but a trick of x'es and oh's. I tuned the radio
with one hand, slid patties into buns or bagged fries
with the other, and became the only known carhop
who delivered a six-pak of cones in one trip. At fifteen
I carved my name into the red counter of the Falls
Drive-In, joining thirty years of names etched back

on June days playing the same greasy radio, girls
a breath past fifteen, frying in the same tiny kitchen,
knowing a boy has fallen when he sticks to you
like a tray to a window. And wondering
if – like carhops – only the start of an engine
or the honk of a horn can bring him back.

Man of the House

"A woman *is* her mother.
That's the main thing."
— Anne Sexton, "Housewife"

My mother scrubbed with Joy and Mr. Clean
late at night, just her and the house awake,
surveyed her work over a Lucky Strike,
as my father did, turning basement to den
creating another room to hide in. They could
only imagine the waste it would be to make
love on clean linoleum, splash of Jungle Jake
to a squirt of Dawn, the lost sweat and blood.
I concoct and experiment with Momma See's
magic potions till I find one that shines.
Comet and vinegar, Ivory and Simple Green
Pinesol and Tide. On the stereo "Louise"

eases the housewife in me, awakened
coed to lover. Years ago on campus nights
together we dodged strange headlights
between the alley and its cars, naked
in the April rain. Working out the ghosts
my husband says, floating across the wet
vinyl floor. On his way up to bed
I call out from my spot the glossed
comfort of *Good night* to soothe
the house's settlings as he endures
these pale rooms' untrained turns
in darkness he can't feel his way through.

And if a woman becomes her mother
then a man *is* the space they share

prefab walls like another skin
to knock out and build up again.

When the Search Committee Asks Me To Tell A Little About Myself

I do not say
I like cottage cheese with pretzel rods
or pastrami on Wonder bread hold the mayo
like reading out loud to myself
and red grapes that squirt
don't say I inhaled, a lot.

Don't say how one March afternoon
a Sunday driving stoned with my best friend
in my father's yellow Delta 88 with the brown top
what she called my *Daisy Mobile*
I pierced an ear thick in cartilage
to chase away the munchies,

or say I feel bare
wearing my mother's pearl earrings
my own dotted studs and delicate hoops
worked out of flesh
for the first time in ten years
left behind in a Jif cap on my vanity.

Don't recall how when we stopped
to put in three bucks of premium unleaded
Super America gave away a free loaf
of Wonder bread with every purchase.
Don't tell the committee
that holds the key to my future

we put the bread in the trunk
so we wouldn't be tempted
the loaf a gift to my mother
a morsel of evidence
to disprove our seemingly
wasted days.

But even from the trunk
we smelled it
through the Farm and Fleet spare
through the tan upholstered back seat
and the millions in lost coins
we smelled it.

Through the curls of our smoke
from the makeshift bong
a Mountain Dew can crushed in the middle
poked with a corsage needle
leftover from a homecoming dance
perhaps junior prom, we smelled it.

Parked beside a pond thawed by spring
we pointed our bare toes north out the windows
and rolled Wonder bread balls
two Catholic school girls
whose souls bordered on lost
tossing crusts to the ganders.

Scrubbing

The woman grew old here
a lifetime at this kitchen window
alone over a day's worth of dishes
her half bottle of Southern Comfort
her Lucky boring into the edge of the counter
and below her spot burned ovals
in the archaic flooring
that won't be SOS'ed away.

Along the mop boards I discover a gray hair.
Not our middle-aged carpenter's, I think,
but the dog's, buried among the perennials,
or the husband's or hers.
Waiting at the sink
pretending a family asleep
upstairs as she scoured
or absently looked down the alley
for the sons across town
or the daughter with her eyes,
or recalled the breath of her lover
as she stood in her husband's galoshes
kept for sleet and scrubbing floors.

The town remembers
the ex-shoe factory foreman
chewed up by his outboard
and for ten years his wife
staggered through nights alone
until she couldn't find her way home
knocked on neighbors' doors till she found one
not moved, divorced, or dead
who'd take her in, call her son
who came home to the lawn
gone to seed under the pines
crab apples dried on their branches
to no jellied end.

"Life in These United States"

"Ew," I say, "imagine living in a trailer park next to the freeway."

He says, "People in love inside those trailers."

At the National Fresh Water Fishing Hall of Fame, Hayward, WI

How we ended up here, emerging
from a musky's mouth is a story
only a Wisconsin family can tell.
The mammoth fish hangs above the town

alluring to you since boyhood, driving past
with your father, his World's Greatest
Fisherman cap displayed on the dash
as he connected the map with taverns

offering you all the 3 Musketeers and
change you wanted, but never one-on-one
in the driveway, a snow fort with your initials
carved in its walls, footlongs at the corner

rootbeer stand, the Ferris wheel at dusk,
or even, in this land of lakes, fishing.
We continue his tradition of weekend rides
through three counties, but you give our son

what you wanted most, something strange
and believable as dinosaurs to any five-year-old:
a whale of a fish surrounded by a school
of stone sunnies, crappies, and bluegills.

In this October desertion, we visit the fish
and the museum, Smithsonian of the midwest,
shrine to a gentle craft of birch canoes and row
boats, cane poles and rods fitted at their ferrules.

Behind glass fishing journals nest among nets, jigs,
flies, chuggers, diamond sinkers, and treble hooks,
gewgaw of my girlhood but to you unfamiliar relics.
One last time you race our son up three flights

through the belly of the World's Largest Fish
two Jonah's who spit from its teethy balcony
past the jagged stone lure, another mark
on your secret list cast in silence.

Add this to fish stories from the turn
of the century, caught and told
somewhere between pinkies or thumbs
oh, about so big, scrappers and keepers

nibbles through years of dawns and afternoons,
anglers who felt the familiar sink-and-draw
who knew the one that got away, the big one.

Untitled (or What I Hate)

Bullies, smell of wet dog, being mean for no reason, gossip, clutter, big eyeglasses, minivans, ranch style homes, cotton candy, and "Untitled" as a title. Cigar smoke, wool socks, loud music, taste of my blood, complacency, and blackheads. When someone dominates a conversation or drinks out of a milk carton. Warm beer, being afraid, rose perfume, collagen lips, the words *amongst, betwixt, slacks* and *faggot*. Decadence, escalators, carnival rides that go in circles, hairy backs, gory movies, crying babies who can't be comforted. Bloated road kill, plaid, reality TV, dishonesty, obsessions I can't let go, and getting too drunk to think. Runny eggs, sweating, my stretch marks, apathy, anything Avon, eye rolling, and following a driver with a blinker on. Mosquito bites, waiting, porridge, dirty ears, vanity, stale cigarette smoke, my varicose veins, and when people don't say *thank you*. Comb-overs, air quotations, Tupperware with lost covers, and Wal-Mart. When people say *knock-knock* as a greeting in an open door. Days when nothing seems important, bloody meat, being misunderstood, ear hair, kissing noises into a phone, redundancy like *RSVP please*. When people say *think outside the box* to sound creative or *my soul mate* to be romantic. Canned peas, bragging, being tickled past laughing, smell of Pinesol, losing, paper cuts, burnt toast, any good thing that goes on too long.

My Mother, According to Me

My mother kneads dumplings with one hand
cuts up a ten-pound capon with the other
but I wanted a concert pianist, perhaps a soprano
though I'll settle for a bongo woman
some lost female Beat.

My mother never met a person without a kind word
but I wished her quick witted and well read
quoting Dickinson each night
Ample make this bed
instead of *Now I lay me down.*

My mother caresses toddlers to sleep
or calms any infant with one coo
cuddles the down off a chick
talks the paint off a barn without bothering a soul
or nurses the spindliest plant back to life.

She pulls bargains off the rack
faster than a Zephyr across the pains,
or cranks a one-armed bandit till four a.m.
and doesn't miss a note of "How Great Thou Art"
three hours later at morning mass.

My mother tells me in detail
about the most recently condensed
volume from *Reader's Digest*
the heroes, the horrors.
She calls my poetry *my writings*

says I use college words she doesn't know
wonders where I get those ideas
and boasts to her friends all the while
wanting a nurse or engineer or farmer's wife
something tangible she can spell out over cards.

A lifetime accommodates the breach
between what we are and who we are not
hostages without a clue for escape
one end of the rope fraying, Mother,
as I tie myself to you with the other.

Two Houses Over

this couple I know only leaning from porches
flees their efficiency,
broasting in August heat this June,
clanging plates on an upstairs landing
large enough for two re-webbed chairs
and a tuneless guitar.

In her rippled tank top she sips
pre-mixed margaritas from a foam cup.
Unmarried I'd guess,
the serenading he does at dusk
as the waning moon slides forward
his Jimmy Buffet straw hat.

From behind she folds her hands
about his shoulders
as he strums the three chords he knows best,
a warbled "American Pie."
Bye Bye, she hums,
as I creep inside.

Saturn Send-Off

"Loving your Saturn is easy, but we'd like
you to make a more serious commitment."

"Excited?" asks Red, the receptionist, and adds,
"Your first?" She's seen our class of pre-owned
stock before, interlopers who name cars by color
in a world where your vehicle defines you.

Teams appear from glass cubicles.
"Betcher excited," they say, annoying as nuggies,
zealots convinced they're selling us a lifestyle.
Along the wall hang testimonies of clients,

multicultural and many gendered, who didn't feel dumb,
or who left a dealership without a headache, for once,
and a bulletin board of hand written notes from
locals like Felky Bremmer saved by 1-800-SATURNS.

A sales consultant, with the shape and lilt of Sammy
Davis guides us to the Launch Pad. Smarmy
in his after-five-enthusiasm, he offers the first drive
momentous as a shattered hymen, which we decline.

Junior uses the extra time on the color-coded owner's
manual written for a dummy, *No offense*, spends
ten minutes on the driver's side, engineered on
the radical idea that the road's the place for your eyes.

He offers us our "Welcome to the Family pamphlet."
We guess he's a former class clown or neighborhood pest,
not, as he says, horticulturist now selling in the suburbs.
"Excited?" he nods, looking into my husband's chest.

Later the used-car Neanderthal promoted to finance
doesn't use the E-word and we like him, till he calls his ex
the wife as if she's the only one, asks my husband
what he does for a living and takes my check.

Bob, the Daddy-O leader, invites us to a New Owner
Workshop, an after hours BBQ just like down home.
Sorry, I won't be there, I'm too excited to go
and so in my place I'll send my Saturn poem.

For Alex, At Ten

It's time you know some stuff . . .

Our eyes don't go anywhere when we sleep, our eyelids simply cover them. ~ There is no NUKKIE Fairy. We replaced your Nuk with a baseball glove. ~ There is no tooth fairy. I save your baby teeth in my jewelry box. ~ Some people don't know how to tease or to be teased. Beware. ~ Sometimes I plan fun stuff to do so I can hear you tell about it. ~ When you complain, I know you're paying attention. ~ People are sometimes mean for no reason, especially kids, especially girls. ~ "I'm sorry" are magical words. ~ Everything ends: sickness, sadness, warts, homework, anger, even happiness. ~ Nobody knows where eye buggers come from. ~ You're bigger than any spider. Have no fear. ~ When you get hurt, you don't have to hurt anyone back. ~ Homemade cards are saved in Bibles or other special places; most store-bought cards are thrown away. ~ Ghosts exist but they'll never bother you. ~ If you smell good, people will want to be around you. ~ If you're ever afraid for no reason, I'll understand. ~ Saying "no" to people can be a good thing. ~ "Please" opens nearly every door. "Thank you" means it will open again soon. ~ Love lives in the details. ~ I watch you sleep more than you know. ~ I like how you let me sit with you in the big green chair sometimes when it's not too hot and I turn my legs just right so we both still fit. ~ I like it when you call from the next room, "Mom, Mom, Mom," barking like the Flintstones' Dino. I especially like it when you say, "Just wondering where you were."

Love is Anticipation

Stepping out of the shower, he says her name out loud.

Pop Quiz

Describe his oldest pair of shoes. What's his favorite sandwich?
Name two teachers he had crushes on. What gift did he often give
his mother on her birthday? How did he get that scar on his cheek?
What cartoon character prompted his first arousal? (Bonus: Describe)

What is his favorite donut? What do his lips do when he writes?
What instrument did his father play? Name the café he lived above
during college. (Bonus: Who paid the rent?)

Name two of his heroes. As an adolescent, what did he do each time
he was left home alone? Name three of his fears. How did he meet
his first wife? Why does he say he married her? (Bonus: Why did he
really?)

What did he lie about to his grandfather the last time he saw him?
What was his mother's secret? What are the three reasons he might
want to be a woman? What is the first song he danced to with a
girl? What did Julia Connelly ask him do at their first boy/girl party?
(Bonus: How much did he like it?)

Wedding Dance

"I knew the bride when she used to rock'n roll."
– Nick Lowe and His Cowboy Outfit

Guests circle the bride as girlfriends
and sisters take turns dancing
through the center, the bride's

make-over sweated away till
she's a tired twelve-year-old again.
We knew the bride when she practiced

at every Skateland snowball for this,
knew her in backyards twisting
an apple stem till it fell off on the first

initial of a boy she liked. No matter, now,
he wasn't the one. This groom whirls
her around till only lace and wool

separate them as they sway.
She can't see he's balding even on
their wedding night, he can't imagine

this dress a flannel night gown.
Married women know it's close to fairy tale,
this Knights of Columbus or VFW Ball.

They danced their way through weddings
for sisters and neighbors who grew up
a step ahead, swapped patent leather

for K-mart bumpers as drummers shook
dance powder on floors, girls on
the edge of a circle waiting their turn.

All this remains of another Catholic
wedding, the verb becoming a ragged
gerund, how we say *my wedding* like

we say *my birthday*, how in the beginning
no one can imagine the end. Women
who haven't danced like this since

their weddings shouldn't yearn to be
this bride watching her groom ease
the garter from her shy thigh, traces

of cake under her chin as she blindly
throws her bouquet to a half-circle
of bachelorettes, shouldn't want to be lost

in what is always borrowed and new
girls again slipping into tennis shoes
but god help me, I do.

Proposition

A rock farm in Newfoundland and between
us we'll have three tweed jackets. Or a houseboat on
the Keys, and we'll sip umbrella'd drinks in
the sun, fish and smoke, grill fillet of
sole over open coals. Or down and out
Down Under we'll slip into anonymity with

catchy pseudonyms, promote readings with
photos of famous dead actors; between
books we'll save whales without
leaving our cottage. Or a greasy spoon on
a baked Phoenix strip of
retirement condos, a napkin in

my flowered lapel. Pearl to your Al, in
The Pink you'll be Dylan with
your Olivia, changing names, of
course, with each stop. Between
cities and countries you'll woo me on
slipping from sleep into one another. Out

shopping you'll hold my purse in your lap outside
the dressing room as you watch inside
the curtain as my shadow slides on
clothes of your choosing we never buy with
cash. At the movies with a jumbo popcorn between
us we'll brush knuckles like we barely know of

each other's past. Over a bottle of
TJ Swan we'll read the Beats by firelight, out
in Super 8 parking lots wedged between
strip malls we'll dance to Patsy Cline, shiver in
goose flesh from rubbing noses. Washing clothes with
one another or sorting recyclables brings on

a slow startle, just like standing on
one foot in line at the IGA, the tousled scent of
my hair in your face. We meet each day with
this reverie, our time measured out
by our bodies' sway, and rise reluctantly into
this day, to this one life between

us, no longer on the outskirts
of a love we want into full time, no longer riddled
with opting between our loving and its savory planning.

Found: Poem

Lost blue parakeet – "Winter"
Very friendly – will not hurt you.
Will sit on head and shoulders.
622 Congress / 839-5114

Escape Fantasies

Saturn dealership, Saturday morning. You're wearing pajama bottoms and your first husband's college sweatshirt. Waiting for your oil change, you eat the complimentary cookies and take a bottle of water for the road. On the complimentary computer, you Google the name of a high school boyfriend. You still have the notebook, social studies or religion, with a list of children's names you thought sounded good with his name. Now you key in his first-middle-and-sur-names. You get 1,479 hits. This search took 20.4 seconds.

~

You find yourself saying to your current lover, *Everyone likes to be invited is all I'm saying.* You both know you're saying much, much more. You know you'll stay the night; still, you want him to ask you. Before bedtime you dance in the kitchen to George Jones. *What my woman can't do can't be done*, he sings in your ear. You know it'll take awhile to be somewhere else.

~

You have silver tracks forming on your ass and thighs. The first time you see one you scrub that spot raw and then buy special lotion. Elasticity, you think, not age. Elasticity can be improved, stretch marks can disappear. Each time you're in an airport you wish you were thinner. Perhaps this is the only time you watch people, and then for a day want to be someone else. You settle for getting highlights like on the woman in seat 12 E.

You have lunch with your best friend from elementary school. You haven't seen each other for so long it's like you're acting out a personal ad. *Divorced white female seeking blast from the past; likes pina coladas and getting caught in the rain.* She has hobbies, says she loves bingo, and plays it every chance she gets. She even has her own collection of dobbers: green, yellow, red, and blue. You can't stop thinking of the rainbow in her purse.

~

I'm a pal to weirdos, your lover says. *Like Jesus was.* You imagine your life without him, imagine you go to the women's room and disappear out the window. This always takes place in the bar where you met, where he first told you *If this isn't a bar you're going to kiss me in then it's no good to us.* You think that these thoughts keep you normal, hold you fast to life as you know it. You return from the bathroom, sit close beside him. There are times to be spontaneous, you think. And tomorrow isn't one of them.

All She Ever Wanted

A bath she could finish, a man who makes
his own casserole, an oven she would use
reluctantly, a novel big enough for two.

SCREENED

Nothing She Ever Wanted

A house she'd have to hide in
a man who wouldn't let her
a child so much like her.

A man she could hide in
a child who didn't like her
a house she had to keep.

A child who hid from her
a man she liked
a house she couldn't leave.

Rewinding the Wedding Tape

The seventh anniversary gift is wool.
I taste it after our wedding tape tradition
when I stay to rewind alone.
Everyone dances off the altar
and I can't hear the *man and wife*
our priest says that in marriage
a schoolboy and waitress become.

In reverse every notion of ceremony
is a motion away, an easy glimpse
of undoing as they return
their rings to the bearer,
the groom's lips un-vowing
the reverted bride's left idle.
They hobble up the aisle.

Walking backwards no one can bear
to lead, her trousseau becomes
an untied knot of satin and lace
the eight foot veil is more a waiting
shroud ungathered like this by attendants.
Chaplin in borrowed shoes, the groom
steps back to rescind his bride.

There's me as I remember me
unhanded by a snare of roses
just for a moment at this inverted
beginning, my new end,
wedged between parents and two exits
given back to myself.

Inamorata

Early at the rendezvous
waiting in desire the hue of dusk
she thinks of all the names
the world could give her.

Squeeze or babe or sideline
trollop or hussy or dish
vamp or wench or moll
not something opulent and serenely

Victorian like lover
or sultry and mysterious like mistress.
She can't recall if she's ever taken off
her shoes when they've loved.

She remembers the names
he has given her: *Exquisite,
My dove, My have to have*
three breaths and her name, three sighs.

O yes. That one time.
When he played Morrison and read Neruda
in the borrowed apartment
the fern weeping to the floorboards

the mail piled up under the slot
the cat mewing at her back
their socks in the corner's dim convergence balled.

Rapture of the Deep

In our marriage bed
I dream of pebbles cool as dimes
smooth from purling water
passed from my mouth to yours.
Your tongue discerns the engraved truths:
Love, Beauty, Fair Play
offered back uneasy as a first kiss.

A man appears beside us in bed
curls to me like an eel.
I slip the pebbles lightly on his tongue
a transition slick as a pirouette.
He flips the pebbles against his teeth like Chicklets
and recites lines from a poem:
The heart that holds what the hand cannot
then *Blossoms when the trees are bare*
and *Only the mouth that asks for more.*

He offers the pebbles back to me
like oranges under the chin at a block party.
The first pebble he blows into smoke rings
that circle my tangled hair,
the next becomes a molar bloody with roots
that clinks in a waiting spittoon,
last is ice on my tongue
burning as it melts.

Dumplings, A Family Recipe

See the new wife's spread of Sunday
dumplings, how a young husband overlooks
her perch swimming in scales and garlic
or a month of Betty Crocker hotdishes.

Mothers teach daughters how a good wife
feels out equal amounts of potato and flour
that dumplings are fool proof, just
knead until you can't knead no more.

In the beginning it's all done for love
then even the dumplings are guilty.
See him line potatoes on his table
as they become conspirators in dumplings.

Mothers advise about courting ignorant
boys, but see how she woos another
woman's husband who knows only
the easy paste of Bisquick dumplings.

See the grocery bag at his feet
catch scraps of evidence as he peels
and she puts out remnants of eyes,
no dark spots for first time dumplings.

See her mash potatoes by hand, one sock
off, a leg on his chair, her skirt hiked
to the knee. See him plump dough
with the flat of his hands, lucky dumplings,

so unlike bread with its instinct for leaven.
See their dumplings sink in boiling water
and teach themselves to rise. See her
later alone at her stove when she finds

there's only so much magic in the world.
See the husband after years with her
how he wants them to taste like his mother's,
ladled with gravy, the same each time.

See her dumplings flop after two days away
or a week of working late, too little flour or
lumpy potatoes, when any dumplings say
for a weary wife, *I am here, and we are fine.*

What We've Seen: Bayfield, Wisconsin

At What Goes Around, a used bookstore, we hear the proprietor refuse boxes of romance novels from a woman in her eighties. After she walks out the front door into her husband's idling Cadillac, he says to us, "Life's too short. It's bad enough I have to sell fiction." We all laugh. If we lived here, you and I'd invite him to our party.

Sailboats in the marina, all of them white but two. We take the ferry across the bay to Madeline Island. We count seagulls, you point out two cormorants, swat biting flies the size of moths. We walk the sidewalks and beaches: candy store, t-shirt shop, condo, more beach, condo, shi-shi restaurant.

We settle for happy hour at Tom's Burnt Down Café – no permanent walls or roof, just a wood frame with a tarp over the bar and sheet metal to block the wind. The lounge area is built up with old car tires and van seats for chairs, a kid's fort made out of whatever's in the garage. The coffee can tip jar on the bar says "Drug Money," behind the bar: "Volunteer Slavery." Everywhere are slogans, sayings, mottos. We read the walls, the floor, the wooden bar top.

"It's like walking into your notebook," you say to me. One or the other of us points and reads:

We're all in the gutter but some of us see the stars. ~ You don't stop laughing because you grow old, you grow old because you stop laughing. ~ It doesn't take a mason to make potato salad. ~ If you act like a dumbshit they will treat you as an equal. ~ Life begins when you get one. ~ Just because a guy doesn't remember what he said doesn't mean he didn't mean it when he said it. ~ I may have been born yesterday but I've been up all night. ~ It's bad luck to be superstitious. ~ Another redneck for peace.

What We've Seen: Bayfield, Wisconsin

The locals have nicknames like Killer or Bomber. It's 3:30 in the afternoon and they're fresh off a construction job, clothes covered in plaster and paint or grease. One turns to you and says, "I know we've met but I don't remember your name." You won't tell him it's your first time on the island. You shake hands and almost spill my beer. I introduce myself. "I'd remember you," he says close to my face. He smells of beer and cigarettes and sweat.

He's with the paraplegic guy we saw when we walked in. The guy's head is shaved but for a flop of bright metallic gold over his forehead. He sits smoking in his electric wheelchair. He's missing a foot and has a withered hand draped on one armrest, nubs where his fingers should be. He's wearing nylon sweatpants, a t-shirt that reads *Though I walk through the valley of death I fear no evil because I'm the meanest mother fucker in the valley*, four earrings in each ear, and a terry cloth bib.

We order another round. I comment on the sun going down on us. You say, "That's how I like my sun: on my back while I'm sitting in a bar drinking."

"Burned one day and tanned the next," I say. "That's how my skin works."

"Put that on a wall," you tease. Instead I write it in my notebook.

What We've Seen: Bayfield, Wisconsin

That night from our balcony we see again the same middle-aged
woman in a matching red pantsuit and hat carrying blue milk crates
full of something. We can't make out the contents, and last night
we were curious but now it's driving us crazy. She sets her wares on
a picnic table under a gazebo and then just sits there. Is she selling
something? Waiting for someone? Holding a picnic dinner? We
can't stand the suspense. After much arguing over who should go, I
pad over to the gazebo in your sandals, sunburned, tired, drunk and
curious. I wave to you when I get to the street.

Even from the curb I can see that the crates are filled with antique
gas lanterns or, most likely, replicas. "Are you selling these?" I ask. I
notice the burnt wicks. I want more details to bring back. I know you
are watching me.

April Rain

It doesn't matter if it's not love,
you say, always aloud, imagining yourself
with him, blinding intimacy
a breath away. In every episode it's raining.
Your husband snores as you chain cigarettes.
In thirty years a sturdy companion

is all you'll want, rockers on porches. It comes
down too quickly to that lovely
girlhood tune. Still, you smell him, his cigarettes
on your hands as your husband tells himself
his day. You live inside yourself, uneasy as rain.
Some nights you dream details too intimate

to record, or you recall past intimacies:
hair drying to curls on his collar, coming
at once, that one time. Only the rain
knows the obscurities love
brings. Later you tell yourself
this time it's over. Swear off cigarettes

and booze with no regrets
until he's drunk and you see intimacy
as he rationalizes to himself,
as loyalty faithfully becomes
lies. Yet with him no doubt it's for love,
and you believe it like you know rain

will stop. In memory it's always April rain,
though afterward when he reaches for cigarettes
across your breasts it's September. Leaving,
you plan conversations only mates
confide: not babies together but what'll become
of the children you'll leave for each other. Selfish,

you blink it away. By yourself
on your stoop you breathe in the rain,
afraid to go inside, too much like company
now. So you light another cigarette
to cover his musk that has mated
with yours. Say again deception is not love.

By next week you're not sure yourself, but rain
streaks the windshield as he comes to meet you, regrets aside,
and shadows lovely on your bodies like tattoos mating.

Couple

Away from him she dwells
on what she's crudely done
Bowling or trigonometry,
she wishes this were one.

She imagines his nylon shirt
name stitched over the pocket
midnight sweat stains in baby blue,
his X'es where she shows single digits.

Or she's an ellipsoid and he sees cusps
or an isosceles to his parabola
or calculator to his abacus on which
one plus one always equals zero.

They have no pictures together
no relics to pack away
no future testimonies of a past
just the pose in the motel mirror

him at her neck, hair loosely
together, another vectored pair's
unsolvable riddle by
faithless affinity squared.

Passing

your wife in the van
as she chauffeurs
your sons to lessons
I tune the radio, imagine
she's smiling, humming
a Carpenter's tune
that one from your wedding.
All this coming and going
make our lives near misses
appointments absently kept
upon this same frayed road.
At home you're still warm from
a one-day January thaw,
chicken falls from the bone
your fork coaxes nudgingly
a Duraflame log glows on the fire.
Your wife turns into the driveway
the motion light guides her key
inside, the table's set to woo us.

Thighs Like Fresh Peaches

When you lay your bag of groceries on the wooden bar top, your milk and bread and fruit remind you that you have parents and children, somewhere.

Each bartender knows your face by what you drink, and this one sets a mug of beer before you and a shot for him. You are a couple only here, this place with pool cues in a barrel in the middle of the barroom and Bessie Smith on the jukebox.

The regulars guess the secrets you keep together, know from the way you walked in tonight – snow-caked scarves and steamed glasses – the songs you'll play again and again standing shoulder to shoulder, as close to dancing as any public place allows.

You chose the fruit together at a corner grocery store. He held each piece to his nose, turned each one round in his hand and said, "We've never shopped for real groceries together." A melodrama only you and he appreciate. You held the fruit to his face and rubbed the fuzz to his cheek. You started to whisper, "Winter thighs like mine."

Handbreadth Away

These fingers too rarely just mine
lacing Batman boots
affectionately picking lint
sewing buttons, kneading dumplings
turning last week's ham to soup

too rarely wandering with yours
in March's ungloved thaw
too often a forced hummingbird wave
at the stoplights as you turn left
and I grope for a cigarette.

Fingers never forget
the crook of your thumb
the swirl of your ear
the creases of your laughing
your scar's parted river of taut flesh.

Once I crossed fingers for luck
to ward off demons and boy germs
or snapped them to an unheard beat
not finger to thumb
but finger to palm.

Together a gang, a gesture apart
thumb out for a lift, pinky swearing
ringer with its teethy diamonds
middle guy screwing you over
pointer accusing or inching you closer.

Three Cities Away

The shirt he unbuttons
she wants to tell him
was her husband's a life ago.
Here, she wants to say,

this grease stain from the house
on Fall Street when he stood
too close to the Fry Daddy
or the spot on the other sleeve

from when they were students
and she made Wonder sandwiches
frosted like a prize
"I-heart-U" in Plochman's mustard.

Instead she watches
the buttons come undone
dull cat eyes winking
each from its snug slit.

What She Wants to Know

about her is mostly her life
with him, if she still watches
him sleep, puts her lips
to his glass or smells his chair
when he's gone or if she ever did

what she says to him at breakfast
if she traces the lines around his eyes
or curls to him in the dark
what she wears to woo him
or if she ever does.

All She Ever Wanted

No oven
two tubs
a novelist.

About the Author

Patti See teaches developmental education and women's studies courses at the University of Wisconsin-Eau Claire. She also supervises tutoring programs for multi-cultural students, students with disabilities, and first-generation/low-income students. Her work has appeared in *Salon Magazine*, *Women's Studies Quarterly*, *Journal of Developmental Education*, *The Wisconsin Academy Review*, *The Southwest Review*, as well as other magazines and anthologies. Her book *Higher Learning: Reading and Writing About College*, 2nd edition, co-authored with Bruce Taylor, was published in 2005 by Prentice Hall. She was the recipient of the 2004 Excellence in Performance Award from UW-Eau Claire.

About the Artist

Todd Clercx lives in St. Paul, Minnesota with his wife, Krista, and three children. He teaches art at Roseville High School. His paintings are a tool for recording his life: emotions, landscapes, people, places, events and moods of everyday routines that are meaningful to him and his family. View more of his work at http://www.tclercxart.com/